Atkins Diet

Atkins Diet Cookbook for Ultimate Weight Loss

Includes Quick and Easy to Cook Recipes

James Houck

COPYRIGHT 2017 - ALL RIGHTS RESERVED

CONTENTS

INTRODUCTION TO THE ATKIN'S DIET

Atkin's diet is one kind of diet which demands in one's lifestyle. If you are not a person who is health conscious then you might need to bring a tremendous change in your lifestyle. Firstly, you must acquire equipment's which are needed to reach your set weight goals. Secondly, you will require some tools like journals to guide your food habits and a guide to counting the carbohydrate intake. Lastly, not to forget, you should consult your doctor to check what suits you the best.

Atkin's diet is a simple and easy diet where you just must reduce your carbohydrate intake. A weight loss program becomes easier only when going on a low-carbohydrate diet. This is well explained in Atkin's diet.

If you eat less of carbohydrates and eat as much protein and as much fat as you want, you can lose weight easily. This will lead to various types of improvement in health.

The most feared saturated fat is also recommended by this diet. Studies have shown that saturated fat is harmless. This diet is better than low-fat diets. The reason for a low-carb diet is that protein intake reduces food consumption while keeping you full for long hours and hence reduces weight easily.

Like other diet's, Atkin's diet also involves its own risks and benefits.

- BENEFITS of this diet are – loss of weight, cardiovascular health improvement, and improvement in good cholesterol, blood sugar, triglycerides and other important health points.

- RISKS of this diet are – Reduction in carbohydrate intake and lack of fiber may cause dizziness, headache, fatigue, weakness, constipation, legs and calves may experience pain when you lay down. The risks are common and the body balance will be back soon. Meanwhile, you can try Vitamin B12 and a fiber supplement to reduce fatigue and ease constipation. So, before you start the diet, just count the carbs in a food using the food nutrition label on the food packet, the dietary fiber, and subtract both. Also, check for any sugar alcohols. Lastly, choose products based on Atkin's diet and foods approved by Atkin's diet.

FOUR PHASES OF THE ATKIN DIET

There are 4 phases in Atkin's diet.

1. INDUCTION (PHASE 1) – this phase is a very important phase in Atkin's diet.
   a. It helps your body start metabolizing the fat stored. You will lose fat as much as 15 pounds or 6.8 kilograms in about two weeks of starting the diet only if you have more than 100 pounds to lose. Else, you will lose around 4-6 pounds normally. If you have consumed a lot of unhealthy foods, then you would probably not fall sick during this phase of dietary change.
   b. One should consume less than 20 grams of carbohydrates a day for first two weeks.
   c. You can consume high-protein, high-fat leafy vegetables. This will induce weight loss right away.
   d. You can choose to take 5-6 small meals a day, as 3 meals will not yield much.
   e. You can snack on during mid-morning and mid-afternoon to fulfill your cravings.
   f. Ensure proper water intake and monitor well.
   g. First, ten days of the diet is very crucial as you may not survive it and decide to revert to your previous lifestyle.
2. BALANCING (PHASE 2) – Firstly, decide if you are ready to move to the second phase before starting it.
   a. Add five grams of carbohydrate to your weekly intake. You will continue to lose weight but at a slower pace.
   b. You can start eating some nuts, fruits, and soft cheeses at this stage.
   c. Reduce your carbs intake to 25 grams if adding 30 grams stops your weight loss.
   d. If you face constipation, increase the water intake and increase fiber intake.
   e. Stick to your diet and balance your sugars.
   f. If you are ordering meals at restaurants, then order Atkin's diet-friendly meals.
   g. To avoid your carbs cravings, plan your meals well.
   h. Vitamins and minerals intake should be well balanced.

3. FINE-TUNING (PHASE 3) –
   a. You should start this phase of your diet when you are just 10 pounds away from your weight loss goal.
   b. You should start adding more carbs to your diet now.
   c. Just ensure you don't add all carbs at once. Just start adding carb food one by one.
   d. Consume varieties of carbs.
4. MAINTENANCE (PHASE 4) –
   a. At this stage, do not stop the diet. Just add healthy carbs to your diet and maintain your weight.
   b. The amount of carb intake should be well balanced.
   c. Lastly, keep a check on your weight regularly.

You may find this plan a bit complicated. You can choose to skip the induction phase and add more fruits and vegetables right from the beginning. This procedure is quite effective as well.

Some choose to stay in the induction phase forever. Such diet is known as very low-carb ketogenic diet (keto).

FOODS TO AVOID

When following a diet, it is very important to know what foods are allowed in the diet. Similarly, Atkin's diet demands its followers to avoid some foods listing down here.

1. GRAINS - rice, wheat, barley, and rye.
2. SUGARS - Fruit juices, soft drinks, cakes, ice cream, candy, and others.
3. VEGETABLE OILS - corn oil, soybean oil, canola oil, cottonseed oil etc.
4. DIET AND LOW-FAT FOODS - high sugar content is found in such foods.
5. TRANS FATS - processed foods contain such fat under the name tagged "hydrogenated".
6. HIGH-CARB FRUITS - apples, bananas, oranges, grapes, and pears. (induction only)
7. HIGH-CARB VEGETABLES - turnips, carrots, etc. (induction only)
8. LEGUMES - chickpeas, beans, lentils etc. (induction only)
9. STARCHES - sweet potatoes, potatoes etc. (induction only)

FOODS TO EAT

Atkin's diet requires its followers to eat the kinds of healthy foods mentioned down here.

1. PHASE 1 – During this phase, you can eat
    a. All kinds of fishes including sardines, herring, salmon, tuna, sole, flounder, and others.
    b. All kinds of fowl including chicken, goose, duck, quail and others.
    c. All kinds of shellfish including crabmeat, clams, mussels, shrimp, squid and others.
    d. All kinds of meat including beef, bacon, lamb, pork, ham and others.
    e. Eggs in all forms including fried, deviled, omelets, scrambled, poached, hard-boiled, soft-boiled etc.
    f. Fats and oils – olive oil, coconut oil, butter, mayonnaise, canola oil and others.
    g. Artificial sweeteners – stevia, sucralose, and saccharine. Each packet includes 1 gram of carbs.
    h. Beverages – club soda, heavy and light cream, decaffeinated tea and coffee, herb tea, water etc.
    i. Cheese and vegetables, salad garnishes, herbs and spices, and salad dressings.
2. PHASE 2 – depending on your readiness, you can continue in phase 1 for more than two weeks.
    a. Add dairy products – mozzarella cheese, ricotta cheese, heavy cream, yogurt, unsweetened whole milk.
    b. Nuts and seeds – walnuts, almonds, pistachios, peanuts, pecans, cashews etc. Also, add their butter in your diet.
    c. Fruits – raspberries, blackberries, cranberries, strawberries, cantaloupe etc.
    d. Juices – lime juice, tomato juice and lemon juice.
    e. Cooked or canned legumes – kidney beans, lentils, lima beans, pinto beans, navy beans, black beans, chickpeas etc.

3. PHASE 3 – you can include the following foods in your diet at this stage.
    a. Fruits – coconut, figs, cherries, watermelon, pomegranate, papaya, plum, guava, apple, kiwi etc.
    b. Starchy vegetables – beets, carrot, peas, acorn squash, butternut squash, baked sweet potato, etc.
    c. Grains – raw wheat bran, wheat germ, oat bran, whole wheat bread, dry polenta etc.

4. PHASE 4 – the foods included in phase 3 are the same for phase 4. Just ensure that you keep a check on your weight gain and the carbs intake. Maintain your lifestyle with Atkin's diet and continue it for your lifetime to manage your health.

WHAT TO DRINK?

A diet is not complete without enough liquids. So, what all can you drink on this diet?

1. WATER - most important ingredient of a diet. Drink as much as you want.
2. GREEN TEA - this healthy beverage accelerates your weight loss.
3. COFFEE – a high number of antioxidants makes this beverage a healthy beverage to consume.

You can also consume small amounts of alcohol - dry wine without sugar. Try to avoid beer which has high carbohydrate content.

Vegetarians can also follow this diet but it is very difficult. Soy-based foods can help you get enough proteins and nuts and seeds will help you include saturated fat content in your food.

Coconut oil and olive oil are good sources of saturated fats from plants.

Lacto-ovo-vegetarians can eat eggs, butter, cheese, heavy cream, and other dairy foods containing high-fat.

BREAKFAST, LUNCH, AND DINNER RECIPES

BREAKFAST RECIPES

SPINACH EGG:
SERVING SIZE: 1 BOWL
SERVINGS PER RECIPE: 1
CALORIES: 194 PER SERVING
COOKING TIME: 5 MINUTES
INGREDIENTS:

1. 2 Whole large Eggs
2. 1 Tbsp. Olive Oil, Extra Virgin
3. 3 cups Baby Spinach
4. Salt to taste
5. Freshly ground pepper

NUTRITION INFORMATION:

1. Saturated Fat - 5.364 g
2. Sugar - 3.2 g
3. Protein - 13.7 g
4. Carbohydrates - 18 g
5. Total Fat - 23.69 g
6. Sodium - 189.51 mg
7. Fiber - 1.44 g

DIRECTIONS:

1. Heat a skillet over medium heat. Add oil and spinach. Sauté the spinach until it wilts.
2. Now add the eggs to skillet. Scramble both the eggs and spinach together and continue the same till the eggs are set.
3. Season it with freshly ground pepper (black) and salt to suit your taste buds.
4. Serve and enjoy.

COCONUT OIL STIR FRIED VEGETABLES AND EGGS
SERVING SIZE: 1 BOWL
SERVINGS PER RECIPE: 1
CALORIES: 527 PER SERVING
COOKING TIME: 10 MINUTES
INGREDIENTS:
1. 2 Tbsp. Coconut Oil
2. ½ cup Baby Spinach
3. 1 cup mixed vegetables
4. 2 whole eggs
5. Spices or just salt and pepper

NUTRITION INFORMATION:
1. Saturated Fat - 26.784 g
2. Sugar - 6.19 g
3. Protein - 20.69 g
4. Carbohydrates - 28.18 g
5. Total Fat - 38 g
6. Sodium - 222 mg
7. Fiber - 6.35 g

DIRECTIONS:
1. Place a frying pan over high heat and add coconut oil.
2. Add the vegetables. If frozen, then thaw it on heat for some time. Else, just sauté for a few seconds.
3. Now add the eggs, spices, and spinach.
4. Stir fry the mixture until done.
5. Serve and enjoy.

BELL PEPPERS ON GROUND BEEF
SERVING SIZE: 1 BOWL
SERVINGS PER RECIPE: 1
CALORIES: 459 PER SERVING
COOKING TIME: 10 MINUTES
INGREDIENTS:

1. 2 Tbsp. Coconut Oil
2. 1 cup Onion chopped
3. 1/4 cup Ground Beef
4. 1 cup Spinach
5. Spices or Just Salt and Pepper
6. 1 medium Red Bell Pepper

NUTRITION INFORMATION:

1. Saturated Fat - 26 g
2. Sugar - 8 g
3. Protein - 10.24   g
4. Carbohydrates - 31.38 g
5. Total Fat - 36.65 g
6. Sodium - 65 mg
7. Fiber - 4.9 g

DIRECTIONS:

1. Place a frying pan on the stove and turn on the flame high.
2. Put coconut oil, onion and stir for 2 minutes.
3. Add the ground beef.
4. Add the spices and spinach.
5. You can add ground pepper and some chili powder for a spicy flavor.
6. Stir fry the mixture until everything is cooked well or ready to eat.
7. Serve hot with sliced red bell pepper.
8. Enjoy.

STUFFED AVOCADO
SERVING SIZE: 1 AVOCADO PER PERSON
SERVINGS PER RECIPE: 4
CALORIES: 464 PER SERVING
COOKING TIME: 20 MINUTES
INGREDIENTS:

1. 4 oz. salmon, smoked
2. 4 avocados
3. 8 small eggs
4. Black Pepper, freshly cracked
5. Salt to taste
6. 1 tsp Fresh Dill
7. Chili Flakes to taste

NUTRITION INFORMATION:

1. Saturated Fat - 1.10 g
2. Sugar - 0.56 g
3. Protein - 14.48 g
4. Carbohydrates - 0.81 g
5. Total Fat - 39.83 g
6. Sodium - 348.5 mg
7. Fiber - 13.5 g

DIRECTIONS:

1. Preheat the oven at 425-degree Fahrenheit or 200-degree Celsius.
2. Cut the avocados in half and deseed them. Just scoop the center bit by bit to ensure it can hold the egg.
3. Now take the avocados and place them on a cookie sheet in line. In the hollows of the avocados, place the smoked salmon.
4. Crack open the eggs one by one into a small bowl and scoop the yolk along with some egg white based on the quantity the avocado hollows can hold.
5. Sprinkle salt and pepper on the eggs as per taste.
6. Now place the avocados in the preheated oven. Bake for around 15-20 minutes depending on the oven.
7. Sprinkle fresh dill and chili flakes on the top.
8. Serve when warm.
9. Enjoy.

WAFFLES (LOW CARBS)
SERVING SIZE: 1 FULL WAFFLE
SERVINGS PER RECIPE: 1
CALORIES: 153 PER SERVING
COOKING TIME: 10 MINUTES
INGREDIENTS:

1. 1 whole egg + 2 egg whites
2. 2 Tbsp. unsweetened almond milk or any other milk of your choice
3. 2 Tbsp. coconut flour
4. ½ tsp baking powder
5. 1 packet Stevia or any sweetener as per taste

NUTRITION INFORMATION:

1. Saturated Fat - 3.5 g
2. Sugar - 3.23 g
3. Protein - 17.2 g
4. Carbohydrates - 12.98 g
5. Total Fat - 7.403 g
6. Sodium - 230 mg
7. Fiber - 5.625 g

DIRECTIONS:

1. Take the 2 egg whites and whip it using an egg beater or a hand mixer or do it manually. Ensure you have stiff peaks.
2. Now add coconut flour, baking powder, milk, sweetener, and the one whole egg.
3. Take your waffle iron and heat it to high temperature.
4. Now grease the waffle iron or spray it with a non-stick spray.
5. Once the iron is ready, pour the waffle batter and cook until the waffle is brown.
6. Remove from the iron and serve it with your favorite topping.
7. Enjoy.

EGGS AND BACON
SERVING SIZE: 1 BACON AND EGG
SERVINGS PER RECIPE: 2
CALORIES: 350 PER SERVING
COOKING TIME: 12 MINUTES
INGREDIENTS:

1. 2 ⅔ oz. sliced bacon
2. 4 eggs
3. Fresh Parsley (Optional)
4. Cherry Tomatoes (Optional), halved

NUTRITION INFORMATION:

1. Saturated Fat - 8.14 g
2. Sugar - 1.16 g
3. Protein - 26.2 g
4. Carbohydrates - 4.45 g
5. Total Fat - 15.41 g
6. Sodium - 356.3 mg
7. Fiber - 0.9 g

DIRECTIONS:

1. Take a pan and heat it on medium flame.
2. Now add the bacon and fry it until crispy.
3. Remove and set aside on a plate.
4. You can now fry the eggs in the bacon grease or separately as per your taste.
5. Fry the cherry tomatoes along with eggs.
6. Serve eggs and bacon with cherry tomatoes.
7. Enjoy.

ALMOND PANCAKES
SERVING SIZE: 4 PANCAKES
SERVINGS PER RECIPE: 1
CALORIES: 300 PER SERVING
COOKING TIME: 5 MINUTES
INGREDIENTS:

1. ¾ of Large Egg
2. 1/16 cup Blanched Almond flour
3. ⅛ cup whole grain soy flour, dry
4. ½ oz. small or large curd creamed cottage cheese
5. ¼ tsp baking powder (double-acting, straight phosphate)
6. ¼ cup Blueberries, fresh
7. 2 Tbsp. Whey Protein, Vanilla flavor

NUTRITION INFORMATION:

1. Saturated Fat - 2.1 g
2. Sugar - 4.68 g
3. Protein - 61.63 g
4. Carbohydrates - 12.54 g
5. Total Fat - 11.49 g
6. Sodium - 127.75 mg
7. Fiber - 3.13 g

DIRECTIONS:

1. Combine all the dry ingredients - soy flour, baking powder, blanched almond flour, whey protein. Mix well.
2. Beat the egg and pour it into the dry ingredients along with cottage cheese.
3. Mix well until no lumps are found.
4. Take a griddle or skillet and heat it on medium flame. Grease the skillet lightly with canola oil or butter.
5. Pour ¼ of the batter into the skillet. When bubbles appear in the center of the pancake, flip over and cook for 2 more minutes or until it is firm.
6. Repeat the same for the rest of the batter.
7. Serve the pancakes blueberries on the top.
8. Alternatively, you can mix the blueberries to the batter before pouring it onto the griddle or skillet.

OMELET - CAPRESE
SERVING SIZE: 1 OMELET
SERVINGS PER RECIPE: 2
CALORIES: 606 PER SERVING
COOKING TIME: 20 MINUTES
INGREDIENTS:

1. 6 eggs
2. 2 Tbsp. of olive oil
3. 3 ½ oz. cherry tomatoes halved
4. ⅓ lb. fresh mozzarella cheese
5. 1 Tbsp. dried or fresh basil
6. Pepper and salt

NUTRITION INFORMATION:

1. Saturated Fat - 17.27 g
2. Sugar - 2.85 g
3. Protein - 41.31 g
4. Carbohydrates - 6.23 g
5. Total Fat - 41.71 g
6. Sodium - 463 mg
7. Fiber - 0.58 g

DIRECTIONS:

1. Crack open all the eggs into a large mixing bowl. Add pepper and salt as per your taste.
2. Whisk until properly blended.
3. Now add basil and stir again.
4. Slice the cheese.
5. Take a large frying pan and heat olive oil.
6. Stir fry the cherry tomatoes for some time.
7. Now pour the prepared egg mixture or batter on the top of the tomatoes.
8. Wait till the batter turns a bit firm.
9. Now add the cheese.
10. Reduce heat and allow the omelet to set.
11. Remove from the pan.
12. Serve hot and enjoy.

EGG MUFFINS
SERVING SIZE: 2 MUFFINS
SERVINGS PER RECIPE: 4
CALORIES: 280 PER SERVING
COOKING TIME: 25 MINUTES
INGREDIENTS:

1. 1-2 medium scallions
2. 6 eggs
3. 3 ½ oz. shredded cheese
4. 4-8 thin slices of salami or air-dried chorizo or cooked bacon
5. 1 Tbsp. green or red pesto (optional)
6. Pepper and salt

NUTRITION INFORMATION:

1. Saturated Fat - 8.99 g
2. Sugar - 0.75 g
3. Protein - 19.59 g
4. Carbohydrates - 1.76 g
5. Total Fat - 19.36 g
6. Sodium - 672 mg
7. Fiber - 0.25 g

DIRECTIONS:

1. Chop the bacon and scallions.
2. Preheat the oven at 175-degree Celsius or 350 degrees Fahrenheit.
3. Crack open the eggs and whisk them with pesto and seasoning.
4. Now add the cheese and stir well.
5. Pour this batter into muffin molds and top it with salami or bacon or chorizo.
6. Based on the muffin forms size, bake it around 15-20 minutes.
7. Remove from the oven.
8. Serve immediately.
9. Enjoy.

HASH BROWNS OF CAULIFLOWER
SERVING SIZE: 3-4-INCH HASH BROWN
SERVINGS PER RECIPE: 4
CALORIES: 294 PER SERVING
COOKING TIME: 30 MINUTES
INGREDIENTS:

1. 3 eggs
2. 1 lb. cauliflower or 16 oz. cauliflower
3. ½ Grated yellow onion
4. 2 pinch pepper
5. 1 tbsp. salt
6. 4 oz. butter, for frying

NUTRITION INFORMATION:

1. Saturated Fat - 15.76 g
2. Sugar - 4.15 g
3. Protein - 7.93 g
4. Carbohydrates - 8.1 g
5. Total Fat - 26.83 g
6. Sodium - 91.5 mg
7. Fiber - 3.2 g

DIRECTIONS:

1. Mix all the ingredients together in a large bowl except the cauliflower.
2. Clean the cauliflower and cut it into long thin pieces as much as required and add this to the mixture already prepared.
3. Set the mixture aside for around 10 minutes.
4. Take a saucepan and heat it on medium flame. Melt a good amount of butter.
5. Now pour a handful of the prepared cauliflower mixture in the frying pan and flatten the mixture carefully. The flattened mixture should be of 3-4 inch thickness.
6. Fry each hash brown for about 5 minutes on both sides and try not to burn them.
7. Flipping the hash brown too early might break them. You can keep the cooked hash browns in the oven to keep it warm.
8. Remove from the pan.
9. Serve with spicy butter or mayonnaise and some leafy greens. You can also serve it with some side dish of your choice.

EGGS AND STEAK WITH SEARED TOMATOES

SERVING SIZE: 1
SERVINGS PER RECIPE: 4
CALORIES: 184 PER SERVING
COOKING TIME: 15 MINUTES
INGREDIENTS:

1. 1 pound flank steak
2. 1 tbsp. + 1 tbsp. olive oil
3. 4 tomatoes, medium, halved
4. Pepper and kosher salt
5. 4 eggs, large
6. 1 tbsp. fresh oregano, chopped

NUTRITION INFORMATION:

1. Saturated Fat - 15.76 g
2. Sugar - 4.15 g
3. Protein - 7.93 g
4. Carbohydrates - 8.1 g
5. Total Fat - 17.72 g
6. Sodium - 140 mg
7. Fiber - 1.8 g

DIRECTIONS:

1. Mix ½ tbsp. of salt, ¼ tbsp. of pepper and steak and toss it well.
2. Take a large skillet and pour 1 tbsp. of olive oil. Heat it on medium-high flame.
3. Cook the seasoned steak for about 5 minutes for a rare-medium. Remove it from the heat and allow it to cool for 5 minutes. Slice.
4. Cook the tomatoes in the skillet till it browns. Cook with the cut side down for 2-3 minutes.
5. In the meantime, on medium flame, heat the tsp of olive oil which is left over in another non-stick skillet.
6. Now crack the eggs into this skillet and cover it. Cook till done. If you want sunny side up eggs, then cook for 2-4 minutes.
7. Sprinkle oregano, ⅛ tsp of salt and ⅛ tsp of pepper on the eggs and tomatoes.
8. Serve eggs and tomatoes with steak.
9. Enjoy.

LUNCH RECIPES

ZUCCHINI PASTA AND POACHED EGGS IN CHERRY TOMATO BASIL SAUCE
SERVING SIZE: ¼ OF WHOLE SERVING
SERVINGS PER RECIPE: 4
CALORIES: 418 PER SERVING
COOKING TIME: 15 MINUTES
INGREDIENTS:

1. 4 zucchinis', medium sized
2. 4 Eggs, Poached
3. 1 ½ pint cherry tomatoes or heirloom cherry tomatoes
4. 4 oz. freshly grated parmesan cheese
5. ⅓ cup sun-dried tomatoes, oil-packed
6. 2 tbsp. pine nuts, toasted
7. 1 cup fresh basil leaves, chopped + for serving
8. 4 tbsp. olive oil
9. 1 garlic clove, grated or minced (optional)
10. ⅓ cup minced Kalamata olives
11. Juice of one lime
12. ¼ - ½ pound of angel hair pasta/spaghetti or more zucchini
13. A pinch of red pepper flakes, crushed

NUTRITION INFORMATION:

1. Saturated Fat - 9.96 g
2. Sugar - 3.815 g
3. Protein - 21.86 g
4. Carbohydrates - 14.83 g
5. Total Fat - 31.96 g
6. Sodium - 648.41 mg
7. Fiber - 4.98 g

DIRECTIONS:

1. Take a large pot of water and add salt. Bring to a boil.
2. In the meantime, mince a pint of cherry tomatoes and place it in a bowl. Add the sundried tomatoes while keeping the oil.
3. Add the basil, lemon juice, garlic, and crushed red pepper flakes.
4. Season the mixture with salt and pepper as per your taste.
5. Set the mixture aside and let it sit for a minimum of 10 minutes.
6. Cook the pasta in boiling water per package instructions and drain.
7. Spiralize the zucchini using a spiralizer and place it in a large bowl. Toss in the hot pasta which is drained of water and allow the zucchini to cook a bit in hot pasta.
8. Now add olive oil, Kalamata olives, and a pinch of pepper and salt. Toss the mixture well.
9. Divide the pasta into 4 portions. Place it in 4 bowls or plates. Pour the tomato sauce on the pasta and placed one poached egg on each plate/bowl.
10. Sprinkle parmesan cheese and the pine nuts.
11. Now break the poached egg placed on pasta and toss the pasta to create the sauce.
12. Add some more parmesan cheese and basil.
13. Serve and enjoy.

SPAGHETTI SQUASH NOODLE AND PEANUT LIME SAUCE
SERVING SIZE: ¼ OF WHOLE SERVING
SERVINGS PER RECIPE: 4
CALORIES: 688 PER SERVING
COOKING TIME: 25-30 MINUTES
INGREDIENTS:
FOR SQUASH:

1. 4 Stem removed Kale stalks
2. 1 large spaghetti squash, deseeded + halved lengthwise
3. 1 shallot, peeled
4. 3 tbsp. sesame seeds
5. ½ cup cashew nuts, toasted (or any other nuts of your choice)
6. 1 bunch broccoli, florets
7. Leafy herb, chopped (mint, basil, cilantro, any other herb - optional)
8. Pepper + Salt

FOR PEANUT LIME SAUCE:

1. 2 garlic cloves, peeled and roughly chopped
2. ½ inch ginger, peeled and roughly chopped
3. 2 tbsp. of peanut butter (or any other butter of your choice like tahini, almond butter etc.)
4. 1-2 tbsp. sriracha (or any other hot sauce of your preference)
5. 1 tbsp. rice vinegar
6. 1 lemon, peeled and chopped
7. 1 tbsp. tamari soy sauce
8. 2 tbsp. agave nectar
9. Extra virgin coconut oil, a small scoop
10. ½ cup grapeseed oil
11. ¼ tsp toasted sesame oil

NUTRITION INFORMATION:

1. Saturated Fat - 10.14 g
2. Sugar - 13.12 g
3. Protein - 15.69 g
4. Carbohydrates - 45 g
5. Total Fat - 47.68 g
6. Sodium - 411.8 mg
7. Fiber - 6.93 g

DIRECTIONS:
1. Preheat the oven to 190-degree Celsius or 375-degree Fahrenheit.
2. Take the halved squash and place it on a baking sheet lined with parchment. Bake it for half an hour or until the flesh can be pulled out in easy strands.
3. Meanwhile, when the squash is being baked, cut the kale leaves into ribbons of a ⅓ inch and put it in a large bowl.
4. Halve the shallots and then slice these halved shallots thinly and set aside.
5. Chop the toasted nuts and herbs and set them aside along with shallots.
6. Cut the broccoli. Take a medium sized saucepan with half an inch of water and bring it to a boil. Lower the heat and simmer. Now place the broccoli florets in a steamer basket and set it aside till you serve.
7. Blend all the sauce ingredients well in a blender. Taste it for seasoning and set aside.
8. When the squash is warm or cooled down enough to handle but not cold, put the broccoli steamer basket into the simmering water.
9. Close the lid of the pot and cook the broccoli for about 3-4minutes or until done.
10. Scrape the strands of spaghetti using a fork into the large bowl containing kale ribbons.
11. The squash heat should be such that it should be able to wilt the kale a bit.
12. Pour the dressing generously. Now season it pepper and salt and toss the squash-kale mixture lightly.
13. Take the broccoli of the heat and divide the squash-kale mixture into 4 bowls.
14. Top each bowl with broccoli, shallots, nuts, sesame seeds, herbs and some extra sauce.
15. Serve and enjoy.

VEGETABLE AND AVOCADO STUFFED "SUSHI" ROLLS
SERVING SIZE: 1 PIECE
SERVINGS PER RECIPE: 2
CALORIES: 455 PER SERVING
COOKING TIME: 10-12 MINUTES
INGREDIENTS:

1. 1 Avocado
2. 2 Organic raw sushi nori sheets
3. ¼-½ Organic red bell pepper, cut into very thin strips
4. ¼ organic zucchini, cut into very thin strips
5. ¼ organic carrot, cut into very thin strips
6. ½ cup sprouted alfalfa (you can use any other sprouts of your choice)

FOR SECRET SAUCE:

1. 1 tbsp. of Dijon mustard (you can use hot, sweet or any other mustard as per your wish)
2. 2-4 tbsp. of nutritional yeast (or as per your taste)
3. 1-2 tbsp. of low sodium tamari sauce, gluten free (or coconut amino)
4. 1 tbsp. organic cilantro, chopped finely
5. 1 tbsp. lime juice
6. Pepper and salt to taste

NUTRITION INFORMATION:

1. Saturated Fat - 2.52 g
2. Sugar - 4.25 g
3. Protein - 16.85 g
4. Carbohydrates - 60.2 g
5. Total Fat - 18.48 g
6. Sodium - 994 mg
7. Fiber - 13.2 g

DIRECTIONS:
1. First get the secret sauce ready.
2. Take all the ingredients under the secret sauce section of ingredients in a small mixing bowl and mix well until a creamy paste is formed.
3. If the texture is too thick, you can use water or lime juice to make it thin. Alternatively, if it too thin, then the more nutritional yeast will help to make the sauce thicker.

NOW THE SUSHI ROLLS:
4. Place the nori sheets on the countertop or a flat surface.
5. Take the avocado, clean, deseed, cut and mash it. Set it aside.
6. Take half of the secret sauce and spread it on the part of nori sheet which is nearest to you.
7. On the spread secret sauce, spread half the mashed avocado.
8. Place the carrots, red bell peppers, and zucchini on the top of the spread mashed avocado horizontally. This should be parallel to the nori sheet edge.
9. Now top it with sprouted alfalfa or any other sprouts of your choice.
10. Now start rolling the edge of nori sheet where you have spread your filling and continue until no filling is visible and it reaches the other end of the sheet.
11. Wet your hand with water and stick the other end of the nori sheet using your wet fingers. The sheet will stick to each other only if the sheet gets damp.
12. Stick the wet end of the nori sheet with the rest of the roll and complete your sushi roll.
13. Repeat the same with the other nori sheet.
14. You can also top with sesame seeds if you wish or use the remaining secret sauce as a dip.
15. Serve and enjoy.

ASPARAGUS AND CHICKEN LEMON STIR FRY
SERVING SIZE: ¼ OF THE WHOLE SERVING
SERVINGS PER RECIPE: 4
CALORIES: 402 PER SERVING
COOKING TIME: 20-25 MINUTES
INGREDIENTS:

1. 1.5 pounds of chicken breasts, skinless and cut into 1-inch cubes
2. ½ cup chicken broth, reduced sodium
3. Kosher salt as per taste
4. 2 tbsp. soy sauce, reduced sodium
5. 2 tbsp. water
6. 2 tbsp. cornstarch
7. 1 tbsp. grapeseed or canola oil, divided
8. 6 garlic cloves, chopped
9. A bunch of asparagus with trimmed ends and cut in 2-inch pieces
10. 1 tbsp. ginger
11. Black pepper as per taste
12. 3 tbsp. lime juice

NUTRITION INFORMATION:

1. Saturated Fat - 4.13 g
2. Sugar - 2.44 g
3. Protein - 53.73 g
4. Carbohydrates - 8.01 g
5. Total Fat - 6.13 g
6. Sodium - 666 mg
7. Fiber - 2.9 g

DIRECTIONS:

1. Season the chicken breasts with light salt and set aside.
2. In a small bowl, combine soy sauce and chicken broth.
3. In another bowl, take water and add cornstarch and mix well.
4. Take a wok and heat it on high flame. When hot, add a teaspoon of the oil and asparagus. Cook until crisp for about 3-4 minutes.
5. Now add the ginger and garlic and cook for a minute more. Set it aside.
6. Take the same wok and on high flame, cook half of the chicken in another teaspoon of oil. Cook till it turns brown and continues till completely cooked. 4 minutes every side is required to cook it completely.
7. Remove the cooked chicken and set aside. Repeat the same with remaining half of chicken and oil. Set aside.
8. Take the soy sauce and chicken broth mixture while bringing it to a boil and cook for 1 to 1 ½ minutes.
9. Now stir in the lime juice, cornstarch mixture and stir well. Simmer.
10. Now add the cooked chicken and cooked asparagus to the sauce and mix well.
11. Take it off the heat.
12. Serve and enjoy.

BARBECUE CHICKEN COBB SALAD
SERVING SIZE: ¼ OF THE WHOLE SERVING
SERVINGS PER RECIPE: 4
CALORIES: 343 PER SERVING
COOKING TIME: 30 MINUTES
INGREDIENTS:

1. 2 thin slices of chicken breasts, boneless and skinless
2. 2 bacon slices, diced
3. Black pepper and kosher salt
4. 2 eggs, large
5. 3 tbsp. BBQ sauce, use more if required
6. 6 cups romaine lettuce, chopped
7. 1 avocado, cleaned, deseeded, and diced
8. 2 diced Roma tomatoes
9. 1 cup canned black beans, drained and rinsed
10. 1 cup can corn kernels, drained

FOR BUTTERMILK RANCH DRESSING:

1. ¼ cup plain Greek yogurt
2. ½ cup buttermilk
3. ¼ cup sour cream
4. ½ tbsp. dried parsley
5. ½ tbsp. dried dill
6. ¼ tbsp. garlic powder
7. Black pepper and kosher salt, as per taste

NUTRITION INFORMATION:

1. Saturated Fat - 4.34 g
2. Sugar   - 9.02 g
3. Protein - 16.44 g
4. Carbohydrates - 33.91 g
5. Total Fat - 16.03 g
6. Sodium - 458.3 mg
7. Fiber - 6.81 g

DIRECTIONS:

1. For buttermilk ranch dressing - whisk together all the ingredients mentioned under the ingredients for buttermilk ranch dressing in a small bowl and set it aside.

2. Heat a large frying pan over medium to high heat. Now cook bacon for around 8 minutes until it turns crispy and brown. Transfer this to a plate lined with paper towel. Set aside.

3. Season the chicken breasts with some pepper and salt as per taste. Cook this in the frying pan until done. Cook at least 4 minutes on one side and flip it and cook for 4 minutes more.

4. Allow the chicken to cool and dice into pieces of bite size.

5. Take a medium sized bowl, combine chicken and BBQ sauce and toss well. Keep it aside.

6. Cook the eggs in boiling water for a minute in a large saucepan. Cover the pan with eggs using a tight lid and take it off the heat. Set aside for 10 minutes before cooling. Once cooled, peel and dice the eggs.

7. In a large bowl, take romaine lettuce. Now top this with BBQ chicken, bacon, tomatoes, eggs, corn, avocado, and beans in well-arranged rows.

8. Serve with the already prepared buttermilk ranch dressing.

9. Enjoy.

PALEO RAINBOW SALAD
SERVING SIZE: ¼ PER PERSON
SERVINGS PER RECIPE: 4
CALORIES: 790 PER SERVING
COOKING TIME: 30 MINUTES
INGREDIENTS:
FOR ALMOND CRUSTED CHICKEN:

1. 1 cup almond flour or leftover from making homemade almond milk or coconut flour.
2. 2-4 chicken breasts, skinless
3. 1 egg, beaten
4. 1 tbsp. of spices, as per your choice
5. Black pepper and sea salt

FOR BALSAMIC ROASTED BRUSSELS:

1. Olive oil
2. A large bag of Brussels sprouts
3. Black pepper and sea salt
4. Balsamic glaze

FOR SALAD:

1. Carrots, shredded
2. 1 head romaine lettuce, finely chopped
3. Corn, raw
4. ½ avocado
5. Halved cherry tomatoes
6. Paleo almond crusted chicken, sliced
7. Balsamic Brussel sprouts, halved
8. Vinaigrette dressing, any

NUTRITION INFORMATION:

1. Saturated Fat - 3.64 g
2. Sugar - 14.17 g
3. Protein- 85.51 g
4. Carbohydrates - 52.57 g
5. Total Fat - 26.45 g
6. Sodium - 289.5 mg
7. Fiber - 13.32 g

DIRECTIONS:

1. For almond crusted chicken - first, preheat the oven at 400-degree Fahrenheit.
2. Take a large baking sheet and line it with aluminum foil and set it aside.
3. In a large bowl, mix the almond flour, spices, salt, and pepper well.
4. In another bowl, crack and whisk an egg well and dip the chicken into the egg mixture until completely coated on all sides.
5. Now dip this chicken into the almond flour mixture until coated on all sides.
6. Place the coated chicken on the ready baking sheet. Set aside.
7. Meanwhile, take the Brussels in a zip lock pouch and drizzle some olive oil. Toss the sealed pouch until the Brussels are completely coated with oil.
8. Take these Brussels onto the baking sheet with chicken and sprinkle with salt and pepper.
9. Bake the chicken and Brussels together for about 15 minutes depending on the oven or until the Brussels start to become soft.
10. Now switch the oven to "Broil". Take off the baking sheet.
11. Sprinkle the Brussels with balsamic glaze. Place the glazed Brussels on the top shelf for broiling. Broil it for only a few minutes only till it is charred slightly and browned.
12. Spoon out the Brussels and set aside. Once cool, halve them.
13. Switch the oven back to bake mode. Bake the chicken for 10 more minutes or until done. Remove and slice it when cool.
14. Take a large salad bowl and layer the bottom with romaine lettuce.
15. You can either create sections or place veggies, almond crusted chicken, and Brussel sprouts in arranged rows.
16. Serve and enjoy.

CANNELLINI BEAN, BROCCOLI, AND CHEDDAR SOUP
SERVING SIZE: 1 CUP
SERVINGS PER RECIPE: 6
CALORIES: 152 PER SERVING
COOKING TIME: 20 MINUTES
INGREDIENTS:
1. 1 cup water
2. 14 oz. can chicken or vegetable broth, reduced sodium
3. 6 cups broccoli crowns, trimmed and chopped
4. ¼ tbsp. ground white pepper
5. ¼ tbsp. salt
6. 14 oz. can cannellini beans, rinsed
7. 1 cup extra sharp cheddar cheese, shredded

NUTRITION INFORMATION:
1. Saturated Fat - 4 g
2. Sugar - 2 g
3. Protein- 11 g
4. Carbohydrates - 15 g
5. Total Fat - 7 g
6. Sodium - 558 mg
7. Fiber - 6 g

DIRECTIONS:
1. In a medium saucepan, combine water and broth and bring it to a boil on high heat.
2. Add broccoli, cook covered till soft. It takes around 8 minutes.
3. Now add the beans, pepper, and salt and cook till the beans are hot, around a minute.
4. Take half of the above mixture and half of the cheese and puree it.
5. Pour the puree into a bowl. Repeat the same procedure for the remaining broccoli and cheese.
6. Serve warm and enjoy.

CAULIFLOWER "COUSCOUS"
SERVING SIZE: 1
SERVINGS PER RECIPE: 1
CALORIES: 626 PER SERVING
COOKING TIME: 20 MINUTES
INGREDIENTS:
1. 1 large cauliflower head
2. 1 cup sun-dried tomatoes
3. 2 cloves of garlic, minced
4. 1 cup leek, sliced thin
5. 1 tbsp. grapeseed oil
6. Pepper and sea salt

NUTRITION INFORMATION:
1. Saturated Fat - 3.9 g
2. Sugar - 23.7 g
3. Protein- 24.4 g
4. Carbohydrates - 85.1 g
5. Total Fat - 30.2 g
6. Sodium - 565 mg
7. Fiber - 28.8 g

DIRECTIONS:
1. Take some water and soak the sun-dried tomatoes. Allow it to rehydrate.
2. Now pulse the cauliflower in a food processor till it resembles couscous.
3. In a cast iron frying pan or skillet, sauté the leeks and garlic on medium to low heat. Continue doing it for some more minutes.
4. Now, remove the rehydrated tomatoes from water and chop it roughly into small pieces. Put this in the frying pan. Cook till the leeks turn soft.
5. Now add the prepared couscous till warm and soft. Be aware that you should not overcook the couscous as it will become mushy.
6. Season with pepper and salt as per your taste.
7. Serve and enjoy.

COURGETTE FRIES WITH DIPPY EGG
SERVING SIZE: 1 PORTION
SERVINGS PER RECIPE: 2 PORTIONS
CALORIES: 222 PER SERVING
COOKING TIME: 37 MINUTES
INGREDIENTS:

1. 1.5 oz. of grated parmesan cheese
2. 2 small Courgette/zucchini, approximately 120 grams each
3. 1 egg, whisked lightly
4. 1 tbsp. parsley, chopped
5. A Pinch of pepper and salt
6. 2 large eggs

NUTRITION INFORMATION:

1. Saturated Fat - 6.07 g
2. Sugar - 2.82 g
3. Protein - 19.12 g
4. Carbohydrates - 5.49 g
5. Total Fat - 13.77 g
6. Sodium - 443 mg
7. Fiber - 1.35 g

DIRECTIONS:

1. Preheat your oven to 400-degree Fahrenheit or 200-degree Celsius. Put the parmesan and egg in 2 shallow dishes, separately.
2. Slice the zucchini/Courgette into pieces of finger size. Dip every piece in the egg, then in parmesan cheese and put it on the baking sheet. Continue the same for all slices of Courgette. Once the slices are ready, sprinkle leftover parmesan if any on the Courgette slices.
3. Sprinkle some seasoning - pepper, and salt. Bake it for about 15 minutes and then reduce the oven temperature to 325-degree Fahrenheit or 170-degree Celsius.
4. Now flip the fries and cook the other side for around 8 to 12 minutes depending on the oven until the fries are golden brown.
5. Meanwhile, cook the 2 eggs in a saucepan. Once done, remove from water.
6. Serve it with Courgette fries immediately.
7. Enjoy.

GREEK CREAMY ZUCCHINI PATTIES
SERVING SIZE: 6 PATTIES
SERVINGS PER RECIPE: 4
CALORIES: 390 PER SERVING
COOKING TIME: 40 MINUTES
INGREDIENTS:

1. 2 pounds or 8 large zucchinis
2. 2 large handfuls of fresh herbs
3. 2 large eggs
4. 3.8 oz./1 cup almond meal
5. 1 tbsp. ground cumin
6. 5.3 oz./1 cup crumbled feta cheese
7. 1 tbsp. sea salt, fine grain
8. 3 tbsp. olive oil, divided
9. Black pepper to taste, ground

NUTRITION INFORMATION:

1. Saturated Fat - 3.41 g
2. Sugar - 12.37 g
3. Protein - 16.96 g
4. Carbohydrates - 27.83 g
5. Total Fat - 27.77 g
6. Sodium - 109 mg
7. Fiber - 10.2 g

DIRECTIONS:

1. Clean the zucchini with water and remove the ends. Grate it on the side holes of a grater or a food processor.
2. Put this grated zucchini in a colander. Sprinkle some salt. Allow it to drain for 10 minutes to 1 hour.
3. Squeeze out the moisture from zucchini using your hands.
4. Take a large bowl and crack open the eggs and beat it. Add the herbs, grated zucchini, cumin, feta, almond meal, pepper, and salt. Mix well.
5. Transfer this egg mixture to a refrigerator for 20 minutes until the almond meal pulls some moisture from the mixture.
6. Remove it from the refrigerator and take small handfuls of the mixture. Form patties.
7. If you feel that the mixture is too wet, add 1 tablespoon of almond meal at a time and mix well.
8. Take a large frying pan on medium to high heat. Once hot, cook the patties for 5 minutes on each side till it turns golden-brown in color.
9. Remove to a paper towel.
10. Serve and enjoy.

GRILLED CORN ZUCCHINI CRUST PIZZA WITH CHIPOTLE BBQ BACON
SERVING SIZE: 2 PIECES PER SERVING
SERVINGS PER RECIPE: 3
CALORIES: 348 PER SERVING
COOKING TIME: 30 + 25 MINUTES
INGREDIENTS:
FOR ZUCCHINI CRUST:

1. 1 egg
2. 4 cups shredded zucchini
3. ¼ cup grated parmesan
4. ½ cup shredded mozzarella
5. Pepper and salt to taste
6. 1 tbsp. oregano

FOR THE PIZZA:

1. ½ cup chipotle BBQ sauce
2. 1 zucchini pizza crust
3. ¾ cup mozzarella or gouda cheese, shredded
4. 4 bacon slices, cut into 1-inch pieces and cooked
5. ½ cup of corn or 1 ear of grilled corn
6. 2 tbsp. cilantro, torn
7. ¼ cup red onion, sliced thin

NUTRITION INFORMATION:

1. Saturated Fat - 9 g
2. Sugar - 15 g
3. Protein - 23 g
4. Carbohydrates - 28 g
5. Total Fat - 17 g
6. Sodium - 986 mg
7. Fiber - 3 g

DIRECTIONS:

1. For zucchini pizza crust - microwave the zucchini on high for about 6 minutes. Allow it to cool. Place it on a tea towel and squeeze out the extra moisture.
2. Mix the egg, zucchini, mozzarella, parmesan, salt, oregano, and pepper.
3. Line a baking sheet with parchment paper and press the above mixture onto the parchment paper.
4. Preheat the oven to 450-degree Fahrenheit or 230-degree Celsius and bake the zucchini crust until it turns golden brown in color. This takes around 15-20 minutes.
5. For pizza - on the freshly baked pizza crust, spread some barbecue sauce.
6. Top this with corn, red onion, bacon, and mozzarella. Bake it until the cheese starts to bubble. This is around 15 minutes.
7. Top it with cilantro.
8. Serve.
9. Enjoy.

DINNER RECIPES

PEPPER AND CHILI BUTTERED STEAK
SERVING SIZE: 1 STEAK PER SERVING
SERVINGS PER RECIPE: 2
CALORIES: 531 PER SERVING
COOKING TIME: 10 MINUTES
INGREDIENTS:

1. 2 Sirloin steaks (175g each), trimmed
2. 50g butter softened
3. 1 tbsp. crushed peppercorns
4. ½ tbsp. wholegrain mustard
5. ½ tbsp. chopped chili in oil
6. ¼ tbsp. salt

NUTRITION INFORMATION:

1. Saturated Fat - 21.81 g
2. Sugar - 0.15 g
3. Protein - 35.74 g
4. Carbohydrates - 0.15 g
5. Total Fat - 42.52 g
6. Sodium - 93.8 mg
7. Fiber - 0 g

DIRECTIONS:

1. Mix the chili, butter, peppercorns, and mustard well. Add very little salt.
2. Take a parchment paper, roll the butter into a cylindrical shape and chill it.
3. In the meantime, using a griddle, cook the steak on both the sides for 3 minutes each to the desired doneness. (You can adjust the timing for well and rarely done).
4. Now remove the well-chilled cylinder of butter and slice it into discs.
5. Place it on the top of steak and serve.
6. You can serve it with some seasonal vegetables or a fresh salad.
7. If there any leftovers, you can store it in a ziplock bag in the refrigerator.

THAI STYLE BEEF IN COCONUT MILK
SERVING SIZE: ¼ OF THE WHOLE SERVING
SERVINGS PER RECIPE: 4
CALORIES: 563 PER SERVING
COOKING TIME: 20 MINUTES
INGREDIENTS:

1. 250g of rice noodles, thick variety
2. 500g of rump steak, stripped
3. 500g packet of stir fry vegetables
4. 250ml can of half-fat coconut milk
5. Juice of 2 limes
6. 2-3 tbsp. red curry paste
7. 2 tbsp. groundnut oil (you can use coconut oil if you want)
8. 1 tbsp. sugar
9. 4 tbsp. fresh coriander, roughly chopped

NUTRITION INFORMATION:

1. Saturated Fat - 6.01 g
2. Sugar - 7.6 g
3. Protein - 32.43 g
4. Carbohydrates - 65.9 g
5. Total Fat - 13.33 g
6. Sodium - 482.3 mg
7. Fiber - 3.2 g

DIRECTIONS:

1. Marinate the steak in red curry paste, sugar and lime juice for 5 minutes.
2. In a frying pan, heat the oil.
3. Add beef to the frying pan and stir-fry for 2 minutes.
4. Now add the coconut milk and bring it to a boil.
5. Cook for 5 more minutes by adding vegetables to the mixture.
6. Meanwhile, cook the noodles separately per the instructions on the packet, drain and set aside.
7. In a bowl take ¼th of the cooked noodles. Spoon some cooked beef from the frying pan and place it on top of the noodles. Sprinkle some coriander leaves.
8. Serve and enjoy.

TANDOORI CHICKEN SKEWERS
SERVING SIZE: 1-2 SKEWERS PER SERVING
SERVINGS PER RECIPE: 6
CALORIES: 658 PER SERVING
COOKING TIME: 60 MINUTES
INGREDIENTS:
1. 500g chicken breast fillets, skinless
2. 6 tbsp. natural yogurt
3. 2 tbsp. tandoori curry paste
4. 1 tbsp. lime juice
5. 1 green pepper, large and deseeded
6. Salt to taste

FOR MANGO SALSA:
1. Lime wedges and boiled basmati rice for serving
2. 1 ripe mango, flesh diced
3. 1 tbsp. lime juice
4. 2 spring onions, chopped finely
5. Salt and pepper to taste

NUTRITION INFORMATION:
1. Saturated Fat - 2.1 g
2. Sugar - 13.64 g
3. Protein - 51.79 g
4. Carbohydrates - 98.28 g
5. Total Fat - 5.32 g
6. Sodium - 524.3 mg
7. Fiber - 3.86 g

DIRECTIONS:

1. For skewers - take the yogurt, curry paste, lime juice, and a tbsp. of salt in a shallow dish (non-metallic). Mix well.
2. Cut the chicken into 1-inch pieces and place it in the yogurt mixture. Toss well for a nice coating.
3. Cover this mixture and let it marinate for an hour at room temperature.
4. Now dice the pepper into squares of small size.
5. Take the (8) metal skewers and thread the pepper and chicken alternately on the skewers.
6. Preheat a grill and cook the skewers under the grill for about 15 minutes. Turn the chicken every few minutes to ensure it is cooked well and charred at places lightly.
7. Meanwhile, make the mango salsa - Take the diced mango, lime juice, spring onions, salt and pepper and mix well.
8. When the skewers are ready, serve it hot with basmati rice, mango salsa, and lime wedges.
9. Enjoy eating.

CHOCOLATE MOUSSE (LOW CALORIE)
SERVING SIZE: 2 MOUSSE
SERVINGS PER RECIPE: 6
CALORIES: 180 PER SERVING
COOKING TIME: 45 MINUTES + COOLING TIME
INGREDIENTS:
1. 60 g skimmed milk powder
2. 160 ml skimmed milk
3. 60 g cocoa powder
4. 4 tbsp. concentrated chocolate essence
5. 13 g granular sweetener
6. ½ tbsp. vanilla essence
7. 90 ml water
8. 11 g gelatin
9. Pinch of cream of tartar
10. 2 egg whites

NUTRITION INFORMATION:
1. Saturated Fat - 1.66 g
2. Sugar - 13.19 g
3. Protein - 18.98 g
4. Carbohydrates - 23.42 g
5. Total Fat - 5.04 g
6. Sodium - 157.33 mg
7. Fiber - 6.66 g

DIRECTIONS:
1. Take and cold milk and skimmed milk powder and whisk well.
2. Warm the prepared milk mixture and add the cocoa powder and whisk well. Allow it cool a bit.
3. Add the vanilla, sweetener, and chocolate essence and mix well. Set it aside.
4. Prepare the gelatin according to instructions on the package. Stir this prepared gelatin into the milk and chocolate mixture already prepared.
5. Allow the mixture to cool and thicken. But do not let it set.
6. Crack the eggs and take only egg whites and the cream of tartar in a separate large bowl. Whisk till it gets firm. Fold this into the ready chocolate mixture taking one spoon at a time.
7. Let it set in the refrigerator.
8. Serve and enjoy.

CHEESE STUFFED BAKED MARROW
SERVING SIZE: 2 MARROWS PER SERVING
SERVINGS PER RECIPE: 4
CALORIES: 366 PER SERVING
COOKING TIME: 25-30 MINUTES
INGREDIENTS:

1. 1 marrow, deseeded and cut into 8 slices
2. 100 g Lancashire or Cheshire cheese, grated or crumbled
3. 50 g mature cheddar cheese or Red Leicester cheese, grated
4. 50 g breadcrumbs, fresh
5. 50 g peas, frozen
6. 50 g sweetcorn, frozen
7. 1 yellow or red pepper, deseeded and chopped
8. 1 small onion, chopped
9. 2 celery sticks, trimmed and chopped
10. 2 tbsp. olive oil
11. 1 tbsp. parsley or fresh chives, chopped
12. Pepper and salt to taste

NUTRITION INFORMATION:

1. Saturated Fat - 8.71 g
2. Sugar - 4.1 g
3. Protein - 19.3 g
4. Carbohydrates - 26.76 g
5. Total Fat - 82.1 g
6. Sodium - 364 mg
7. Fiber - 11.13 g

DIRECTIONS:

1. Preheat the oven to 400-degree Fahrenheit or 200-degree Celsius. Grease lightly a large baking sheet with olive oil.
2. Take a large frying pan and heat the remaining oil. Add onion, pepper, and celery and sauté for about 4 minutes till the celery and onion are soft.
3. Take it off the heat and add peas and sweetcorn. Stir well.
4. Set aside a few tablespoons of breadcrumbs and put the rest into the above mixture, the remaining vegetables, Cheshire cheese, chives and mix well. Season with salt.
5. Line the marrow slices on the prepared baking sheet. Pack the slices with the vegetable mixture. Sprinkle the grated Red Leicester cheese and the breadcrumbs.
6. Cover this with a foil. Bake it for around 20 minutes. Remove the foil and continue baking for 10 more minutes till the top browns.
7. Remove, serve, and relish.

LEEK AND ASPARAGUS SOUP
SERVING SIZE: ¼ OF THE SERVING
SERVINGS PER RECIPE: 4
CALORIES: 156 PER SERVING
COOKING TIME: 15 MINUTES
INGREDIENTS:
1. 1 Leek
2. A 14.5 oz. can of chicken broth, consommé or bouillon
3. ¾ lb. asparagus
4. 2 tbsp. unsalted butter stick
5. 1 tbsp. garlic
6. ⅓ cup heavy cream
7. Salt and pepper to taste

NUTRITION INFORMATION:
1. Saturated Fat - 8.3 g
2. Sugar - 2.94 g
3. Protein - 6.85 g
4. Carbohydrates - 7.77 g
5. Total Fat - 13.3 g
6. Sodium - 391.3 mg
7. Fiber - 2.21 g

DIRECTIONS:
1. Take a large pot and melt the butter over medium to high heat.
2. Sauté the leeks in the melted butter for about 3 minutes.
3. Now add asparagus and cook for a minute.
4. Add garlic to the cooked mixture and sauté for 30 seconds.
5. Add the chicken broth and bring the soup to a boil.
6. Reduce the heat and cover the pot. Simmer for about 10 minutes or until the asparagus is soft.
7. Remove from heat, add pepper and heavy cream and blend it in a blender to a smooth mixture.
8. If the soup is not hot enough, you can heat it well again.
9. Season with pepper and salt.
10. Serve and enjoy.

TUNA KEBABS IN ASIAN STYLE
SERVING SIZE: 1 SKEWER PER SERVING
SERVINGS PER RECIPE: 8
CALORIES: 179 PER SERVING
COOKING TIME: 33 MINUTES
INGREDIENTS:
1. ¾ pound eggplant
2. 32 oz. Tuna, boneless
3. 5 ⅓ Tbsp. tamari soy sauce, gluten free
4. 1 tbsp. toasted sesame oil
5. 2 ⅔ FL oz. rice wine
6. 1 tbsp. ginger
7. 2 tbsp. sucralose based sweetener
8. 3 tbsp. garlic
9. 1 large red sweet pepper
10. 3 large spring onions or scallions
NUTRITION INFORMATION:
1. Saturated Fat - 3.08 g
2. Sugar - 2.03 g
3. Protein - 28.09 g
4. Carbohydrates - 5.93 g
5. Total Fat - 3.13 g
6. Sodium - 644 mg
7. Fiber - 2.1 g

DIRECTIONS:

1. You will need skewers for this recipe. If using bamboo skewers, then soak in water for 15 minutes before use. Else you can use metal skewers.
2. Heat grill to the highest temperature.
3. Take a large bowl and combine rice wine, soy sauce, ginger, sesame oil, garlic, and the sweetener. Mix well.
4. Add the spring onions, tuna, and red pepper and toss until coated completely.
5. Marinate this mixture in the fridge for 15 minutes. After 15 minutes, remove the tuna, red pepper and spring onions from the marinade and set it aside.
6. Now toss the eggplant in the marinade. Allow it sit aside for 3 minutes. After 3 minutes, remove the eggplant from the marinade and set aside along with the rest of the ingredients. You can discard the leftover marinade.
7. Take 8 skewers and start threading. Thread it with 2 spring onions pieces, 3 tuna pieces, 2 red pepper pieces, and 3 eggplant pieces alternatively. Do the same with all the skewers.
8. Ensure that the eggplant is skewered through the skin on both the sides.
9. Now grill the prepared skewers for about 4 minutes on each side. Center of tuna should be rare.
10. Serve the kebabs and enjoy your dinner.

BAKED GOAT CHEESE AND RICOTTA CUSTARD
SERVING SIZE: 1 PER SERVING
SERVINGS PER RECIPE: 4
CALORIES: 365 PER SERVING
COOKING TIME: 55 MINUTES
INGREDIENTS:

1. 1 cup whole milk Ricotta cheese
2. 1 ⅓ canola cooking spray, original
3. 6 oz. semi-soft goat cheese
4. ¼ cup English walnuts, chopped
5. 3 tbsp. grated parmesan cheese
6. 12 spinach leaves
7. 2 tbsp. basil
8. 2 Eggs, whole and large
9. ⅛ tbsp. black pepper
10. ⅛ tbsp. salt

NUTRITION INFORMATION:

1. Saturated Fat - 15.58 g
2. Sugar - 2.49 g
3. Protein - 20.59 g
4. Carbohydrates - 5.39 g
5. Total Fat - 29.36 g
6. Sodium - 416.87 mg
7. Fiber - 1.07 g

DIRECTIONS:

1. Heat the oven at 350-degree Fahrenheit.
2. Take 4 5-ounce custard cups or ramekins and spray the cooking spray.
3. Take a large mixing bowl and combine goat cheese, ricotta, parmesan, basil, walnuts, eggs, pepper and salt and mix well.
4. Line each of the 4 ramekins with 3 leaves of spinach.
5. Divide the cheese mixture into 4 parts and fill each of the ramekin lined with spinach leaves to full.
6. Bake this in the preheated oven for 30 minutes. Remove and cool for 5 minutes.
7. Once cool, run a knife around the edges of the ramekins and invert it onto a plate. Season with pepper and salt as per taste.
8. Serve and enjoy.

BLACKBERRY SPINACH SALAD WITH GOAT CHEESE MEDALLIONS
SERVING SIZE: A PORTION OF THE SERVING
SERVINGS PER RECIPE: 6
CALORIES: 224 PER SERVING
COOKING TIME: 30 MINUTES
INGREDIENTS:

1. 30 cherry tomatoes
2. 12 oz. Blackberries
3. 1 Egg, large
4. ¼ cup half pecans
5. 2 tbsp. extra virgin olive oil
6. ¼ medium red onions, sliced
7. 6 oz. soft goat cheese
8. ¾ tbsp. cinnamon
9. 1 ⅓ tbsp. balsamic vinegar
10. 1 tbsp. Xylitol (sweetener)
11. 9 cups baby spinach

NUTRITION INFORMATION:

1. Saturated Fat - 5.4 g
2. Sugar - 3.4 g
3. Protein - 8.92 g
4. Carbohydrates - 13.55 g
5. Total Fat - 15.39 g
6. Sodium - 157 mg
7. Fiber - 2.6 g

DIRECTIONS:

1. Chop onions and set aside in a bowl.
2. Chop pecans and set aside in another bowl.
3. Crack an egg into a small bowl and whisk well.
4. Roll the goat cheese into 12 flat balls of half inch rounds or cut it.
5. Dip the goat cheese balls in the whisked egg. Roll these in the pecans and press if required.
6. Place it on a baking sheet and bake in an oven preheated at 350-degree Fahrenheit for ten minutes or take a sauté pan and cook the goat cheese medallions over medium to high heat for 5 minutes on each side.
7. Remove and cool a bit.
8. Heat 2 tablespoons of oil in the sauté pan and cook the onion with cinnamon and the sweetener for 3 minutes.
9. Add half of the blackberries into the onion mixture and mash all the blackberries with a fork. Cook for 4 more minutes.
10. Add balsamic vinegar, pepper, and salt, cook for 2 minutes and remove from the heat. Let it cool.
11. You can use this dressing warm or store it in the refrigerator if you want it cooler. This is a thick dressing, so mix water or lime juice if you want it thin.
12. Now mix tomatoes, spinach, and blackberries. Toss this mixture with half of the dressing prepared. Place on a plate and top it with the cheese medallions prepared earlier.
13. Place the remaining dressing on the side and serve.
14. You can serve it with salmon, chicken, or shrimp on the top, if desired.
15. Enjoy.

TURKEY - BLUEBERRY BURGERS
SERVING SIZE: 1 BURGER
SERVINGS PER RECIPE: 6
SMART POINTS PER SERVING: 4
CALORIES: 175 PER SERVING
COOKING TIME: 30 MINUTES
INGREDIENTS:

1. ¾ cup blueberries
2. 1 ¼ lbs. ground turkey
3. ½ cup red sweet pepper, chopped
4. 1 tbsp. light olive oil
5. ¾ cup Feta cheese, crumbled
6. 3 tbsp. peppermint (mint)
7. 1 ½ tsp cumin
8. 1 ½ tsp fennel seed
9. ½ tsp black pepper
10. ½ tsp salt

NUTRITION INFORMATION:

1. Saturated Fat - 2.53 g
2. Sugar - 2.33 g
3. Protein - 25 g
4. Carbohydrates - 4.48 g
5. Total Fat - 6.9 g
6. Sodium - 227mg
7. Fiber - 1.38 g

DIRECTIONS:

1. Take ground turkey, chopped mint, olive oil, ground cumin, ground fennel, pepper, and salt in a bowl. Combine all these ingredients using hands.
2. Add the feta cheese, chopped red bell pepper and blueberries combining gently. Form 6 equal sized burgers. If the peppers and blueberries pop out, you can gently push it back. Add some more pepper and salt.
3. Pan fry or grill the burgers over medium to high heat. Continue frying until the internal temperature is 165-degree Fahrenheit. At this temperature, the center of the meat changes color from pink and the juices are clear.
4. Serve immediately and enjoy your dinner.

LEMON CHICKEN WITH ARTICHOKE HEARTS
SERVING SIZE: ½ LB. OF CHICKEN
SERVINGS PER RECIPE: 3
SMART POINTS PER SERVING: 10
CALORIES: 439 PER SERVING
COOKING TIME: 20 MINUTES
INGREDIENTS:

1. 1 ½ lb. chicken, skinless and boneless, largely diced
2. ½ cup lightly packed basil leaves, sliced thin
3. 1 ½ cups artichoke hearts, quartered (not frozen)
4. 3 medium garlic cloves, sliced thinly
5. ⅔ cup white wine, dry
6. ½ medium yellow onion, chopped finely
7. 2 tbsp. olive oil
8. ⅓ cup water
9. 1 tsp lemon zest
10. 1 tsp fresh lemon juice

NUTRITION INFORMATION:

1. Saturated Fat - 1.99 g
2. Sugar - 12.23 g
3. Protein - 56.04 g
4. Carbohydrates - 13.98 g
5. Total Fat - 11.85 g
6. Sodium - 532 mg
7. Fiber - 2.82 g

DIRECTIONS:

1. Take a large frying pan and over medium to high flame, heat the olive oil.
2. Add garlic and onion. Season it with pepper and salt. Cook until the onion turns golden brown for about 4 minutes.
3. Now add chicken and cook while stirring occasionally. Cook for about 5 minutes or until the chicken turns brown on all sides.
4. Add artichoke hearts. Cook till artichoke hearts start breaking down.
5. Add water, wine, lime juice, and mix well. Ensure no bits are stuck to the bottom of the pan.
6. Cook for 5 minutes or until the wine smell goes away and the sauce thickens lightly.
7. Take it off the heat.
8. Mix lemon zest and basil leaves.
9. Serve and enjoy.

ABOUT THE AUTHOR

James Houck is a health and fitness enthusiast who loves teaching people about healthy ways to lose weight and live the best life they can.

Over the years, he has studied what works and what doesn't in health and fitness. He is passionate about helping others achieve great success in their diet and exercise endeavor through his books and seminars.

His biggest satisfaction is when he finds out that he was able to help someone attain the results they've been looking for. In his free time, he loves to spend time with his 2-year-old daughter.

Printed in Great Britain
by Amazon